OVERFLOWING GRACE

Romans 9, 10, 11 and 15

David N. Jones

The substance of addresses given at the
Evangelical Movement of Wales Annual Conference,
Aberystwyth 2011

BRYNTIRION PRESS

© David N. Jones, 2012

First published 2012

ISBN: 978 185049 245 0

Evangelical Movement of Wales

The EMW works in both Welsh and English and seeks to help Christians and churches by:
- running children's camps and family conferences
- providing theological training and events for ministers
- running Christian bookshops and a conference centre
- publishing magazines and books

Bryntirion Press is a ministry of EMW

Past issues of EMW magazines and sermons preached at our conferences are available on our website: www.emw.org.uk

Published by Bryntirion Press, Bryntirion, Bridgend CF31 4DX, Wales, in association with Evangelical Press, Faverdale North, Darlington, DL3 0PH, UK

CONTENTS

PREFACE

Sometimes people skip over chapters 9–11 of Romans, or put them in brackets, because they are full of difficult and controversial things. I come to these chapters not as a theologian, except in the way we are all theologians, but just as an ordinary pastor who tries to preach to my congregation week by week. There are things in these chapters that I still find difficult to understand – and I am grateful for the help I have received from the writings and preaching of others.

People gather for the Aberystwyth conference over the weekend before the conference proper begins. Providentially, Geoff Thomas's ministry before the conference really set me up to get into these chapters. He preached on the text, *'The secret things belong to the LORD our God, but the things revealed belong to us'* (Deuteronomy 29:29), and he pointed out to us that the truth is not somewhere in the middle; it is at both extremes. We preach what is in Scripture; we do not try to reconcile what God has placed there side by side. When Spurgeon was asked, *'How do you reconcile God's sovereignty with human responsibility?'* he replied, *'I don't try to reconcile friends.'*

These chapters of Romans speak to us not only of the sovereignty of God and human responsibility, but also of the relationship between Jew and Gentile in the purposes of God. In AD 48 the Emperor Claudius kicked the Jews out of Rome, and what began no doubt as a largely Jewish church became predominantly Gentile. In these chapters Paul warns Gentile Christians against arrogance and superiority and, worse than that, anti-Semitism.

'Therefore receive one another, just as Christ also received us, to the glory of God. Now I say that Jesus Christ has become a servant to the circumcision for the truth of God, to confirm the promises made to the fathers, and that the Gentiles might glorify God for his mercy . . .'

(Romans 15:7-9, NKJV)

DAVID N. JONES
Hobart, Tasmania
May 2012

Chapter 1
'How odd of God to choose the Jews!'
Romans 9:1-29

'How odd of God to choose the Jews!' Apparently it was a British journalist by the name of William Norman Ewer who wrote those words many decades ago in the *London Daily Herald*. A response came from Ogden Nash, the American poet: *'But not so odd as those who choose the Jewish God and hate the Jews.'* The Christian Church has not always been blameless when it comes to anti- Semitism. How odd to choose the Jewish God, to believe in the Jewish Messiah, to read the Jewish Scriptures – and to hate the Jews!

Someone else joined in the discussion with these words: *'How strange of man to change the plan!'* That is the real question here in these chapters in Romans. Has there been a change of plan? Is Christianity Plan B? Why did God choose the Jews? And if he did, why is it that, right down to the present day, the Jews, generally speaking, do not believe in Jesus? This is the problem that Paul is dealing with here in Romans. Jewish unbelief may not be high on our agenda today, but it was a major issue for those early Christians.

This matter of Jewish unbelief raises profound questions and stirs deep emotions. Why are some saved, while others perish? Why is it that in our family circles some are saved and others not? This is a question for our hearts as well as our heads, and that is where Paul begins.

Paul's distress

It is a parent's worst nightmare for a child to go missing. Sometimes you read of such things in the newspaper, and you imagine what you might feel in such circumstances. If your child went missing, you would do anything to find that child, wouldn't you? And if you have reason to fear the child is in danger or has come to some harm, your gut instinct is to want to swap places. You say, '*I'd rather it be me than her.*'

That is how Paul feels about his fellow Jews. In this chapter he is going to say some controversial and challenging things, but this is where he begins. His heart is breaking for his people:

> '*I speak the truth in Christ – I am not lying, my conscience confirms it in the Holy Spirit – I have great sorrow and unceasing anguish in my heart. For I could wish that I myself were cursed and cut off from Christ for the sake of my brothers, those of my own race, the people of Israel.*'
>
> (Romans 9:1-4a)

In the heart of Paul there is an echo of what Moses experienced at Mount Sinai. You will remember how, after receiving the Ten Commandments, he came down the mountain to find the people worshipping a golden calf. What an outrageous sin these people had committed: it is like finding your wife in bed with the best man on your wedding day! Moses has been on the mountain, signing the register; God has entered into covenant with his people; and here they are committing spiritual adultery! That is the nature of sin, of course: it is not simply a case of breaking a few rules; it is breaking God's heart, trampling upon God's love. God has brought them up out of Egypt, and he is taking them into the Promised Land.

> 'Moses said to the people, "You have committed a great sin. But now I will go up to the LORD; perhaps I can make atonement for your sin." So Moses went back to the LORD and said, "Oh, what a great sin these people have committed! They have made themselves gods of gold. But now, please forgive their sin – but if not, then blot me out of the book you have written."' (Exodus 32:30-32)

Do you see? Moses is willing to swap places with these people!

Yet what Moses was not permitted – and not able – to do, Jesus actually did! At the cross Jesus took the place of sinners. Paul says he was made sin for us (2 Corinthians 5:21). You name it, he became it: everything that shocks us; everything we recoil from; everything that horrifies us; everything we would be so ashamed for anyone to know about – he became it, he took it all upon himself. Without becoming a sinner himself, he became sin. He was made sin for us. He literally went through hell for us.

God hid his face from Jesus on the cross because of our sin. Paul says he was made a curse for us, for *'Cursed is everyone who is hung on a tree'* (Galatians 3:13).

So do you see what is happening here in these opening verses of Romans 9? The Spirit of Jesus is in Paul yearning over the lost sheep of the house of Israel: *'I speak the truth in Christ – I am not lying, my conscience confirms it in the Holy Spirit – I have great sorrow and unceasing anguish in my heart. For I could wish that I myself were cursed and cut off from Christ for the sake of my brothers, those of my own race, the people of Israel.'*

Ray Steadman, an American preacher, once asked a congregation why they had got rid of their pastor. *'Well,'* they said, *'he kept telling us that we were going to hell.' 'But doesn't your new pastor tell you that?'* asked Steadman. *'Oh yes, he tells us that as well. But when he tells us, unlike his predecessor, it sounds like it's breaking his heart. He's not glad about it.'*

Let me ask you this. When you think of your nearest and dearest, those closest to you who do not believe in Jesus, does it break your heart? We must never allow ourselves to become accustomed to the fact that people who are bound to us by close ties are lost and on their way to hell.

When Paul thinks about his fellow Jews, it fills him with profound personal pain and drives him to his knees. He will go on to say much in these chapters about the sovereignty of God in choosing to save some and not others, and in the face of that some people think, *'If God is sovereign in the matter of salvation, there is nothing we can do about it. So there is no point in praying or evangelising.'* But nothing could be further from the truth. Paul opens up this very subject on his knees, pleading for his fellow Jews, willing to swap places with them if that were possible, so that they might be saved. Some people come to these chapters spoiling for a fight; but that is not the spirit in which Paul writes. He is not looking for an argument; he is agonising over his own flesh and blood. His own people have rejected their Messiah, and that disturbs him very deeply indeed.

Leonard Ravenhill tells the story of Charlie Peace, a notorious nineteenth-century criminal who was condemned to death and executed in Leeds Jail. It was the custom, on a prisoner's last walk to the gallows, for the prison chaplain to walk ahead of him, reading out a particular order of service. Ravenhill describes the chaplain walking ahead of this prisoner, sleepily reading some Bible verses. The criminal asked, *'What are you reading?'* and was told, *'I am reading the consolations of religion.'* Shocked at the 'professional' way this man read about hell, the prisoner preached what Ravenhill calls his 'on the eve of hell sermon'. *'Sir,'* he said to the preacher, *'if I believed what you and the Church of England say that you believe, even if England were covered with broken glass from coast to coast, I would walk over it, if need be, and I would think it worthwhile living just to save one soul from an eternal hell like that.'* Ravenhill asks:

'How could a man be so unmoved under the very shadow of the scaffold, as to lead a fellow human being there, and yet, dry-eyed, read of a pit that has no bottom into which this man must fall?

*Could this preacher believe the words that there
is an eternal fire that never consumes its victims,
and yet slide over the phrase without a tremor?
Is a man human at all who can say with no tears,
"You will be eternally dying, and yet never know
the relief that death brings"?'*

Paul's dilemma

But then, secondly, notice Paul's dilemma. Who are
these people he is so distressed about, and is praying
for so earnestly? They are his people, Jewish people,
God's chosen people. God says to them through Moses:

*'. . . you are a people holy to the LORD your God.
The LORD your God has chosen you out of all the
peoples on the face of the earth to be his people,
his treasured possession. The LORD did not set
his affection on you and choose you because you
were more numerous than other peoples, for
you were the fewest of all peoples. But it was
because the LORD loved you and kept the oath
he swore to your forefathers that he brought you
out with a mighty hand and redeemed you . . .'*
(Deuteronomy 7: 6-8)

This raises for us some big questions. If God has
chosen the Jewish people; if he has made an everlasting
covenant with Abraham to be his God, and the God of
his children after him down through the generations; if
he is going to bless all the nations of the world through
the seed of Abraham – then has God's Word failed?
Has God welched on his deal with Abraham? Here in
chapter 9 Paul wrestles with three important questions:

Has God's Word failed? – Romans 9:6; Are God's ways
fair? – Romans 9:14; and Is God's will free? – Romans
9:19.

Has God's Word failed?

Consider all the privileges and advantages that God had
given Israel. Paul lists eight of them here in verses 4 and
5: the adoption as sons, the divine glory, the covenants,
the law, the temple, the promises, the patriarchs, and the
Messiah himself. If, despite all these privileges, and all
the promises God has given them, Israel is now lost, how
can I be sure that I am going to be saved?

It is a question of assurance, isn't it? At the end of Romans
8 we are told that *'nothing will be able to separate us
from the love of God that is in Christ Jesus our Lord'*
(Romans 8:39). But if Israel is separated from the love
of God that is in Christ Jesus, how can we trust God's
Word? Paul argues:

> *'And we know that in all things God works for
> the good of those who love him, who have been
> called according to his purpose. For those God
> foreknew he also predestined to be conformed
> to the likeness of his Son, that he might be the
> firstborn among many brothers. And those he
> predestined, he also called; those he called, he
> also justified; those he justified, he also glorified.'*
> (Romans 8:28-30)

Well, was not Israel called? Did not God foreknow Israel?
Clearly for these early Christians, most of whom were
Jews, this was a profound pastoral problem. As Paul

went around the Mediterranean evangelising, he always went to the Jews first, but in synagogue after synagogue the door was slammed in his face. Those early Christians might well be asking, *'What is going on? How can I be sure that God will keep his promises? The Jews do not believe. How can I trust his Word if Israel is lost?'*

But it is more than a pastoral problem; it is also a theological dilemma. In becoming Christians, Paul and those early believers had separated themselves from the majority of their fellow Jews. Paul, who was once their champion, had now turned traitor as far as they were concerned. Just think how difficult that must have been for the apostle! He was going in one direction, and everyone else was going in another. What do you do when that happens?

That is how it was in the fourth century for Athanasius, when faced with the Arian controversy that denied the deity of Christ. Bishops, church councils, emperors, magistrates, theologians – they were all going down the same road, and here was Athanasius on his own. *'Nobody believes what you are teaching, Athanasius. The whole world is against you.'* To which Athanasius famously replied, *'Well, in that case, Athanasius is against the whole world.'* And those words became his epitaph: *'Athanasius contra mundum.'*

This is also what Luther faced at the Diet of Worms in 1521, when called to account for his writings and required to recant. The pope did not agree with him; the whole mediaeval church believed otherwise. But Luther stood his ground: *'My conscience is captive to the Word*

of God ... Here I stand; I can do no other.'
When everyone else goes in one direction and you are left standing alone, it is time to consult the map. It is time to go back to the Scriptures to find out if you are on the right track. That is what Paul does here: he opens up his Bible to make sure he is on the right track. What does he find there?

Grace, not race

What Paul discovers in verses 6-9 is that what lies at the heart of God's election is grace, not race:

> *'It is not as though the word of God has failed. For not all who are descended from Israel belong to Israel, and not all are children of Abraham because they are his offspring, but 'Through Isaac shall your offspring be named.' This means that it is not the children of the flesh who are the children of God, but the children of the promise are counted as offspring. For this is what the promise said: 'About this time next year I will return and Sarah shall have a son.'*
> (Romans 9:6-9, ESV)

Just because you have Abraham's DNA does not make you a child of Abraham, and just because you have Abraham's genes does not make you a child of God. Both Jews and Muslims trace their ancestry back to Abraham. Both Isaac and Ishmael were sons of Abraham, but God chose Isaac, not Ishmael, to be the child of promise.

You will recall the remarkable story of Isaac's birth. God made a promise to Abraham that in his seed all the families of the earth would be blessed; but the promise was a long time coming, and as Abraham and Sarah grew older and older, it seemed as if it would never happen. So Abraham took matters into his own hands and tried to force its fulfilment. He had a child through Sarah's 'home-help', Hagar, and Ishmael was born. This was a huge mistake, with long-lasting after-effects. They had to wait for the promise to be fulfilled, and then, just when it looked as if there would be no people of God in the world at all, Isaac was born! It looked impossible, and it was impossible; no wonder Isaac's name means 'laughter'! But that is the way God operates: he takes *the foolish things . . . the weak things . . . and the things that are not*' (1 Corinthians 1: 27-28); it is *'Not by might nor by power, but by my Spirit'* (Zechariah 4:6).

So has God's word failed? No. God never said that that every son of Abraham would believe. It has always been grace, not race. It is not biological Israel but believing Israel that God has chosen, and it is the people who believe the promises of God who are the saved in the Old Testament. They are the true Israel, the Israel within Israel. Just to put that beyond any shadow of doubt, in verses 10-13 Paul takes us down a generation. Isaac's children, Jacob and Esau, were twins; they shared not only the same father but the same mother; they shared the same womb and were probably conceived in the same act of sexual intercourse. There was nothing to decide between them; yet we are told that before they were born, before they had a chance to do anything good or bad, God told Rebekah that the older would serve the younger.

Commenting on this thousands of years later as he reflected on subsequent history, the prophet Malachi wrote, *'Jacob I loved, but Esau I hated'* (Malachi 1:2-3; quoted in verse 13). We must be careful about making those words mean something that is unworthy of God. When Jesus said, *'If anyone comes to me and does not hate his father and mother . . . he cannot be my disciple'* (Luke 14:26), he is using a Hebrew idiom. Jesus – the one who has fulfilled all righteousness – is not going to tell us that we should hate our parents. What he is saying is that it is a matter of preference or priority, a question of who comes first. And that is just what God said to Rebekah: *'The older will serve the younger.'*

So Malachi, as he looks back over a long history, consults the road map of the Scriptures and discovers that it is grace, not race; it is faith, not physical descent. And faith is not a work, not something you conjure up within yourself; it is simply reaching out to what God provides, as a beggar stretches out his hand for bread. Does that make you better than anybody else? Of course not! Was Jacob better than Esau? Far from it! Jacob was obnoxious, a spoilt 'mummy's boy', a cheat and a deceiver. Someone has said that the really surprising thing is not that God hated Esau, but that he loved Jacob. If you read about Jacob (Genesis 25ff.), you will find nothing lovable about him. And there is nothing lovable about us either! In *The Sound of Music*, when Captain Von Trapp proposes to Maria, she sings, *'Oh, somewhere in my life I must have done something good.'* No, that is not why God chose Isaac, or Jacob, or you. It is not because, looking down the centuries, he knew you had the propensity to believe. No, you did not! If you have faith, it is only because God has given it to you. Jews and Gentiles alike, we are all rebel sinners, dead in our trespasses and sins. God saves us by his grace; it is not a work – *'It does not . . . depend on man's desire or effort'* (verse 16), that is, man wanting this or trying this; it is God's undeserved favour. Well, is that fair?

Are God's ways fair?

In verse 14 Paul anticipates the question that will arise. Is it fair for God to deal with people in this way, to show preference, choosing some and passing over others? Is it fair to choose Isaac and not Ishmael, Jacob and not Esau? *'What then shall we say? Is God unjust? Not at all! For he says to Moses, "I will have mercy on whom I have mercy, and I will have compassion on whom I have compassion"'* (verses 14-15).

Mercy, not merit

Maybe you have heard the story of the ageing film star who said to her hairdresser, *'Young man, I hope you are going to do me justice,'* and was told, *'Ma'am, it's not justice you need; it's mercy.'*

Did Israel deserve to be God's chosen people after what happened at Sinai, when Moses came down and found the people worshipping the golden calf? Why did he not wash his hands of them after that outrageous betrayal, and choose another nation to take their place? But what God says in that passage is, *'I will have mercy on whom I have mercy.'* William Shedd preached a sermon on this text entitled *'The exercise of mercy is optional with God.'* That is the character of mercy. Even Shakespeare knew that: *'The quality of mercy is not strained . . .'* Mercy is not something you can demand, nor something God can be forced to show.

The story is told of a rich man who decided to sponsor some inner-city kids to give them a decent education, guaranteeing full college tuition for twenty of them. Now is anybody going to say, 'But that's not fair! I mean, there are hundreds of kids living in the inner city, and he's only going to sponsor twenty of them!'? The man was under no obligation to help any of those children, so the fact that he did so had nothing to do with fairness; it was sheer mercy. Mercy has nothing to do with fairness. It is grace, not race; faith, not physical descent; mercy, not merit. None of us deserves mercy.

In verses 17-18 Paul goes on to cite the case of Moses and Pharaoh. He takes us back to those chapters in Exodus which describe the 'showdown' between God and Pharaoh (Exodus 7–14). Have you ever asked yourself why there were ten plagues – surely it did not take God ten rounds to knock out Pharaoh? We are told: *'For the Scripture says to Pharaoh: "I raised you up for this very purpose, that I might display my power in you and that my name might be proclaimed in all the earth"'* (verse 17). The truth is that God was in that encounter with Pharaoh: in Pharaoh's stubbornness in refusing to do what God commanded him to do, in Pharaoh's hardness of heart and hardening of his heart, God was displaying his power and making his name known. He can make the wrath of men to praise him. Without being the author of evil, he can take evil dictators and evil men, and get glory to his own name. That is what he was doing here. And at the same time as getting a name for himself amongst the nations, he was dealing with this man Pharaoh, giving him space for repentance. These two things may sound contradictory, but they are not; they go together. Ten times in those chapters in Exodus we are told that God hardened Pharaoh's heart; but ten times also it says that Pharaoh hardened his own heart. This is in line with what Paul says in the opening chapter of Romans:

> *'God gave them over in the sinful desires of their hearts to sexual impurity for the degrading of their bodies with one another. They exchanged the truth of God for a lie, and worshipped and served created things rather than the Creator . . . Because of this, God gave them over to shameful lusts . . . Furthermore, since they did not think it worth while to retain the knowledge of God, he gave them over to a depraved mind, to do what ought not to be done.*
>
> (Romans 1:24-26, 28)

'God gave them over': you cannot quarrel with the justice of that, can you? When God hardens people's hearts, he is just giving them over to what they want to do. He simply solidifies what is there already. No one will be in hell who does not want to be there. No one will want to be there once they get there; they will forever regret being there; but no one will be in hell who does not want to go there. That is the scary thing about hell. It is not the London dungeon, or Dante's Inferno, or demons with pitchforks. It is much scarier than that, and much closer to home. You see, what happened here was that Pharaoh was swept into hell by the choices he made.

C. S. Lewis in his book, *The Great Divorce*, teases out what hell is like. This, of course, is literature, not theology, and not the last word on the doctrine of hell. But he talks about the 'grumbler' becoming a 'grumble'. You start off as a bit of a grumbler, thinking at first that you can stand apart from that mood and criticise it. But eventually, as you give in to the mood continually, it takes over, and the grumbler becomes a grumble, until in the end all that is left is a grumble – not a human being any more, but a grumble, just grumbling on for all eternity.

Or here is a man who is addicted to pornography. This is a huge problem today because of modern technology and the ease with which people can get on line. The man makes a decision to access that page on the worldwide web. It is his decision, he presses the button, he is tempted and he views it. Again and again he presses that button, and every time he does so he is making a decision. In the end what does this unclean, lecherous man become? Filth! 'As the tree falls, so it lies.' That is hell. People do not just drop into hell through some trap door that opens; it is much more dangerous than that. Some of you may be on the way to hell right now, because of the decisions you have made. You have been digging your heels in against God's Word, going against your conscience, hardening your heart as Pharaoh did, and the choices you have been making are drawing you to hell.

Pharaoh was swept to hell on the basis of the choices he made. God was patient with him, giving him every opportunity to repent and to change his mind, but over and over again we read that Pharaoh hardened his heart.

Are you hardening your heart? That is a path that leads to destruction. Maybe you are on that path now – and there, but for the grace of God, I would be, and so would many of us, because we are all made of the same stuff. The late great John Stott says this: *'If anybody is lost, the blame is theirs; but if anybody is saved, the credit is God's.'* This antinomy contains a mystery which our present knowledge cannot solve, but it is consistent with Scripture, history, and experience.

So it is grace, not race; faith, not physical descent; mercy, not merit. If you want God to be fair, then none of us would be saved because, as Paul argued, *'all have sinned and fall short of the glory of God'* (Romans 3:23). There is none that does right, no, not one, neither Jew nor Gentile. We are all in the same boat.

Is God's will free?
That brings me to the third question: Is God's will free? 'What about free will?' is the question that is always raised, and again Paul anticipates it. But notice what he says in verse 19: *'For who resists his will?'* It just depends on whose will you are talking about, you see – yours or God's. The question is not *'Do I have free will?'* but *'Does God have free will? Is God free to do whatever he pleases?'* Or, to put it another way, does the world revolve around you, or does it revolve around him? People used to believe that the sun and the stars and the moon all revolved around the earth, and then Copernicus realised that it is the sun that is the centre of the solar system, and the earth revolves around the sun. Do we not need a Copernican revolution in our churches today? C. S. Lewis, in his famous broadcast talk, *God in the dock*, says this:

'Ancient man approached God, or the gods, as the accursed person approaches his judge, but for the modern man the roles are reversed: man is the judge, and God is in the dock. Man is quite a kindly judge: if God should have a reasonable defence for being the God who permits war and poverty and disease, he is ready to listen to it; the trial may even end in God's acquittal. But the important thing is that man is on the bench and God is in the dock.'

Some years ago I saw a cartoon of Jonathan Edwards preaching that famous sermon of his, *'Sinners in the hands of an angry God'.* But the speech bubble in the cartoon showed the preacher's text as *'God in the hands of angry sinners'.* Is not that where we are in today's church? God is answerable to us; it is all about me. Just think about some of the songs people sing. God is there as the heavenly butler: if he does not answer my prayers, I will call him to account; he is there to massage my ego, to make me feel good about myself. The whole thing revolves around me. We need to realise that God is sovereign, that God has free will, that God can do whatever he pleases without having to explain himself to us. *'Who are you, O man, to talk back to God?'* says Paul (verse 20).

Paul uses the picture of the potter and the clay to explain this to us. It is a composite picture taken from Jeremiah and Isaiah. Both prophets were ministering to Israel at the time of the exile, when the people were asking such questions as *'Why has this happened? What is God doing? How could God allow such a thing – for us to be carried into exile?'* In dealing with these issues, both prophets use the same picture.

'Does not the potter have the right to make out of the same lump of clay some pottery for noble purposes and some for common use? What if God, choosing to show his wrath and make his power known, bore with great patience the objects of his wrath – prepared for destruction? What if he did this to make the riches of his glory known to the objects of his mercy, whom he prepared in advance for glory – even us . . .?'
(Romans 9:21-24)

Why did God take his people out of their land and into exile in Babylon? What is the potter doing as he shapes and moulds the clay? We may not all agree with this, but what seems to me to make most sense in the context is that God is shaping his people to be a vessel of mercy – not so much a vessel to receive mercy as to convey mercy. Is not that what he has been doing down through the centuries, ever since the promise made to Abraham?

I know very little about pottery, but I do know that it is a skilled craft. Sometimes the potter has to stop and start all over again, and sometimes he has to break pieces off. That is what God has been doing with Israel; he is doing it especially at the time of the exile – and God is free to do what he wishes. He chose this nation to be his vessel of mercy to the world, to bring the knowledge of God to the rest of mankind, saying to Abraham, *'In your seed all the nations of the earth shall be blessed'*

(Genesis 22:18 NKJV). And just when it looked as if Israel was finished, broken on the potter's wheel, with only a few shards left on the floor, God called the Gentiles – not to replace Israel, but to reshape and remodel her: *'even us, whom he also called, not only from the Jews but also from the Gentiles'* (Romans 9:24). 'Even us' – even descendants of Ishmael and Esau and Pharaoh (and here he quotes from Hosea's prophecy) – *'I will call them "my people" who are not my people; and I will call her "my loved one" who is not my loved one . . . in the very place where it was said to them, "You are not my people", they will be called "sons of the living God"'* (verses 25-26). Even us! We who were *'Not my people', 'Not my loved one'* (Hosea 2) – we who were *'far off, strangers to the covenants of promise'* (Ephesians 2) – now belong where we did not belong before; we have been brought in. We who once were nobodies are now somebody; we who once were not a people are now God's people.

So has God's Word failed? His word to Abraham was: *'I will multiply your descendants as the stars of the heaven and as the sand which is on the sea-shore . . . In your seed all the nations of the earth shall be blessed'* (Genesis 22:17-18 NKJV). Is he not doing that? Do you realise that there are more people alive in the world today than have ever lived in all the centuries of world history before? And God's Word is still powerful and active in the world; the gospel preached to Abraham is still being preached, and the elect are being gathered in. God's Word will not fail. Through the preaching of the gospel he will give Abraham what he promised: more children than can be numbered.

So has God's Word failed? No, he never said he would save every Israelite. But grace is generous; in fact, another word for grace is 'generosity'. It is not the chosen few or the 'chosen frozen'; it is more than can be numbered. God is rich in compassion and full of mercy. He has kept his promise right up to the present time, and his Word is still going out to the nations – 'even us'!

Has God's Word failed? Are God's ways fair? Is God's will free? Can he do whatever he wants? Is he sovereign? Is he ever caught off guard or forced to change his plans or adapt? Does he have to respond and react to us? No! He is absolutely sovereign; he works all things out according to his determinate counsel and purposes.

Paul's delight

We have seen Paul's distress, and we have tried to wrestle with Paul's dilemma; but I want you to see finally Paul's delight in Jesus Christ. There is some questioning about the translation here, but I think the NIV is correct. Paul is speaking of the privileges that belong to Israel:

> *'Theirs is the adoption as sons; theirs the divine glory, the covenants, the receiving of the law, the temple worship and the promises. Theirs are the patriarchs, and from them is traced the human ancestry of Christ, who is God over all, for ever praised! Amen.'*
>
> (Romans 9:4-5)

All those privileges and promises point to Jesus, who is, according to the flesh, the seed of Abraham, the Son of David. Salvation is of the Jews according to the flesh, but he is 'God over all, for ever praised!' Augustine famously puts it like this: *'Without ceasing to be what he eternally was, he became what he eternally was not.'* That is a profound statement. What has he always been? *'God over all, for ever praised',* worshipped by angels, without beginning, without end, the sovereign God! *'Without ceasing to be what he eternally was',* he became just a cluster of cells in the womb of the virgin Mary, no bigger than the dot of a letter 'i'. He grew up in the carpenter's shop in Nazareth. Just think of it: eternity toddling around on little rubbery baby legs, falling over and being picked up! *'Without ceasing to be what he eternally was',* he became a Jew, the seed of Abraham, a descendant of David. He became one of us, a human being. Without ceasing to be God, he became man.

In the Middle Ages, Anselm wrote a very famous book, which became a Christian classic: *Why did God become Man?* The book's thesis is that salvation had to be achieved by God because no one else could do it, and yet its debt was owed by man, so only man could pay it. This is what he says:

> *'It would not have been right for the restoration of human nature to be left undone, and it could not have been done unless man paid what was owing to God for sin. For the debt was so great that, while man alone owed it, only God could pay it; so that the same person must be both man and God. Thus, it was necessary for God to take manhood into the unity of his person, so that he who, in his own nature, ought to pay and could not, should be in a person who could. The life of*

this man was so sublime, so precious, that it can suffice to pay what is owing for the sins of the whole world and infinitely more.'

Why did God become man? For this reason: to live the life that we should have lived but could not, and to die the death that we deserve to die. In other words, the sovereign God of Romans chapter 9 is the God who is in Christ. God was in Christ reconciling the world to himself. He is over all, and he is in Christ. And Paul is saying here in verse 5 that he is worthy of praise. In the end, what lies behind our salvation, and indeed even behind the condemnation of the lost, is the praise of God, and the last word has to be this: *'May Jesus Christ be praised!'*

When Paul thinks about his nearest and dearest who do not believe in Jesus, he is distressed. The depth of his distress challenges our apathy and complacency. But when he thinks of the greatness of Jesus and what he has come to do, he is delighted, and his great passion is to make Christ known, to introduce people from within his own family circle to this all-sufficient Saviour.

Do you have loved ones? Are you losing sleep over them? Are you breaking your heart for loved ones who will not acknowledge Christ? I want to say to you, *'Don't give up!'* Paul did not. Everywhere he went, he went to the Jews first. It is amazing to see his persistence as he travelled around the Mediterranean knocking on synagogue doors and getting thrown out. Paul was no academic Calvinist; his heart was telling him to go to his family.

'But how do I know,' you may ask, *'whether my daughter or my son is elect, or my husband, my wife or my parents?'* You will never know; that is none of your business: *'The secret things belong to the LORD our God, but the things revealed belong to us'* (Deuteronomy 29:29). What has God revealed? He has told us to pray, to pray without ceasing, and to go on praying. Do not puzzle over things that you can never understand. We do not know who the elect are, or how many there are, but we do know that they are more than can be numbered, and we do know that God loves to work in families. So do not puzzle about these things, but pray! Pray and praise! Praise God for what you do understand, for what he has revealed. Praise him for sending Jesus into the world, and delight yourself in him. If you have unconverted children in your home, are they growing up in a home where Jesus Christ is praised? That is the best environment for growing Christians.

Are you unsure whether you are a Christian? Well, you can make sure; you must make sure. John Calvin said, *'Christ is the mirror of our election.'* I think what he meant is this. You do not look anywhere else except to Christ. You do not look in on yourself and become introspective; you do not start taking your spiritual pulse – one day it will be racing, and the next you will wonder whether there is any life there at all. Delight yourself in Jesus; look to Jesus; look into the mirror! Spurgeon said: *'I looked to the cross, and the dove flew into my heart. I looked at the dove, and it flew away.'*

> *I dare not trust my sweetest frame,*
> *But wholly lean on Jesus' name.*

On Christ the solid rock I stand,
All other ground is sinking sand.
Edward Mote (1797-1874)

So look to Christ and delight yourself in him. Make Christ the mirror of your election, and look into that mirror every day. May Jesus Christ be praised!

Chapter 2
The tragedy of unbelief
Romans 9:30 – 10:21

If you are into *The Simpsons*, you will be familiar with Homer Simpson's grace: *'Dear God, we paid for all this ourselves, so thanks for nothing!'* That is irreverent, even bordering on the blasphemous. Yet it is the way many people think about life – even many Christian people, though perhaps they would not articulate it like that. After all, what has God got to do with it? It was my decision, my upbringing, my parents, my Sunday school teacher, the friend who brought me along to church – so thanks, God, for nothing! Is that what you want to say? I hope not.

Here in chapters 9 and 10 of Romans, Paul puts two truths side by side: Divine Sovereignty and Human Responsibility. In chapter 9 we have seen that if anyone is saved at all, it is God's doing, so credit where it is due:

To God be the glory, great things He has done;
So loved He the world that He gave us His Son.
Frances Jane Van Alstyne (1820-1915)

It is God who takes the initiative; it is he who is sovereign in the matter of our salvation; he chooses who will be saved – and it is not because of anything that is in us now, or any potential he may have foreseen. It is purely grace and love; there is no other explanation. It is grace, not race; it is faith, not physical descent; it is mercy, not merit; and it is God's choice, not ours.

But now we come into Romans chapter 10, where Paul is going to argue human responsibility. Why do the Jews not believe in Jesus? Why have they, of all people, rejected their own Messiah? In all his travels Paul's first port of call is the Jewish synagogue; yet almost without exception, as soon as he starts talking about Jesus, the Jews throw him out. Why don`t they believe? Paul gives four reasons, and I want to take you through them and apply them to us, so that we do not make the same mistake ourselves.

Stumbling over the foundation

The first reason is at the end of chapter 9: they had a foundation, but they stumbled over it.

> *'They stumbled over the "stumbling-stone" As it is written, "See, I lay in Zion a stone that causes men to stumble and a rock that makes them fall, and the one who trusts in him will never be put to shame."'*
>
> (Romans 9:32b-33)

It is like assembling a piece of furniture from MFI or IKEA. It comes in a flat pack and there is always a piece left over and you wonder what it's for. Sometimes it's the bit that holds everything together. Without that vital piece everything wobbles and collapses in upon itself. Paul, using a different metaphor, pictures Zion as a construction site. As the workmen busy themselves on the site, they keep tripping over a huge stone. Who put that stone there? Nobody knows what it is doing there or where it came from, so in the end they just toss it out. But it is the cornerstone, and God put it there. And not only did he put it there, but he told them he was going to put it there. It is the keystone in God's plan to save the world, and they have stumbled over it and tossed it aside. Ironic, isn't it? It would be almost comical if it were not so tragic. They have tossed it aside, and the Gentiles – the non-Jews, you and I with no Bible background to speak of, people who are not particularly looking for Jesus – we have stumbled across him.

Do you remember the parable Jesus told about the treasure in the field? The man stumbles across buried treasure, and sells everything in order to buy the field. But the Jews, to whom the field belongs – the Jews who have been waiting for centuries for the Messiah to come and have been carefully prepared for his coming – do not recognise him when he comes and stumble over him.

> *'He came to his own, but his own did not receive him. Yet to all who received him, to those who believed in his name, he gave the right to become children of God – children born neither of natural descent, nor of human decision . . . but born of God.'*
>
> (John 1:12-13)

That is the tragedy of Jewish unbelief. Instead of embracing Jesus as their Messiah, recognising him as God's provision for their salvation, and building their lives on the foundation which God has laid in Zion, they have stumbled over him – he has become a stumbling block to them.

'What then shall we say? That the Gentiles, who did not pursue righteousness, have obtained it, a righteousness that is by faith; but Israel, who pursued a law of righteousness, has not attained it. Why not? Because they pursued it not by faith but as if it were by works. They stumbled over the "stumbling-stone"'.

(Romans 9:30-32)

Picture it as a race - the race for righteousness. It is like a horse race – let's call it the 'Justification Stakes'– and the firm favourites are the Jews. Yet, against all the odds, the firm favourites lose the race; they do not cross the finishing line. *'Christ is the end of the law for righteousness'* (Romans 10:4). That's where the finishing line is, and that's where they should have ended up, but instead they are still on the track, wandering around in circles. And the rank outsiders, the Gentiles, who never even knew that there was a race, have just wandered onto the track and stumbled over the finishing line. Afterwards, the pundits analyse the race and give us the explanation: *'they pursued [righteousness] not by faith, but as if it were by works'* (Romans 9:32). That is the mistake that caused them to stumble. It is a very common mistake.

The default mechanism

When my laptop crashes, it goes back to its 'default' setting, 1 January 1970. The 'default mechanism' of the human heart is Works! I remember one lady, when something tragic happened in her life, saying, *'Why should this happen to me? I've taught Sunday school all my life.'* That is the default mechanism. Works! The trouble with works is that you never get there.

I sometimes tease our cat by training a beam of light onto the wall! The cat just can't help jumping and stretching after it. What Paul is saying here is that the Law is beyond our reach; it is too high; we cannot attain it. Jesus shows us in the Sermon on the Mount that the Law is not just about external behaviour, tidying up our lifestyle; it is about the attitudes of our heart – our pride and vanity, greed and envy. If I want to make myself right, I am never going to be able to do it. But the great news of the gospel is that God has given us in Christ the righteousness that the Law requires of us, a righteousness that is by faith: *'Christ is the end of the law for righteousness to everyone who believes'* (Romans 10:4). The Law of God is holy and just and good; it is a revelation of the righteousness that God requires, and it searches us out and shows us up. But the mistake is to pursue it as if it were a work, something you can attain yourself rather than by faith.

That is the mistake the Jews made. Jesus is the way to get right with God; the Law was never meant to be an end in itself; it was always meant to point to Jesus as its destination. But the Jews stopped at the signpost. The Law was pointing to Jesus, encouraging them to go on to the great provision God was making for their salvation, but they stopped short. Jesus is the only one who has ever kept God's Law perfectly, and he is the only way to get right with God.

The law of the land makes a twofold demand on us: it requires us to keep it, and if we fail to do so we are punished for breaking it. In the same way, the Law of God makes a twofold demand upon us: it requires us to obey, to live perfect lives; and if we do not, then we will be punished. It is as simple as that. Christ is 'the end of the Law' in both these senses. He lived a perfect life of obedience to his Father's will; it was not beyond him or out of his reach; he fleshed it out winsomely and wonderfully, and so he is 'the end of the Law' in that sense. And at the same time he took the punishment of a broken law upon himself: *'Cursed is everyone who does not continue to do everything written in the Book of the Law'* (Galatians 3:10). Jesus took that curse upon himself on the tree, and *'Anyone who trusts in him will never be put to shame'* (Romans 10:11).

How encouraging those words are! When I think about Judgement Day, one of the things I most recoil from is the embarrassment of it: to think of every secret thought, every hidden motive coming out on the Day of Judgement! None of us wants that. But the wonderful thing is this: everyone who believes in Jesus, who calls upon the name of Jesus, will not be put to shame:

> *His perfect obedience and blood*
> *Hide all my transgressions from view.*
> Augustus Montague Toplady (1740-78)

So Israel's failure (if I can put it this way) is Christological: it has to do with their failure to understand who Jesus is. They have stumbled over the stumbling stone, tripped over the keystone in God's plan of salvation. They have missed the righteousness that he alone can bring, and pursued a righteousness that they can never attain. They had a foundation, one that God laid in Zion, but they have stumbled over it. Let us make sure that we do not make the same mistake.

A misdirected zeal

Secondly, they had a zeal that was misdirected. Paul says:

> *'Brothers, my heart's desire and prayer to God for the Israelites is that they may be saved. For I can testify about them that they are zealous for God, but their zeal is not based on knowledge.'*
> (Romans 10:1-2)

Given the choice, whom would you prefer to operate on you, an enthusiastic medical student or a skilled surgeon? Zeal without knowledge can be fatal. Paul himself is proof of that – he was the Osama bin Laden of the Jewish world, *'as for zeal, persecuting the church'* (Philippians 3:6). He separated children from their parents; he destroyed churches; he murdered Christians; he stood by, holding the coats of the men who were stoning Stephen, the first Christian martyr. He was a wide-eyed religious fanatic who sincerely believed that he was doing God's will. But he was wrong. People say, *'It doesn't matter what you believe as long as you are sincere.'* That is absolute nonsense! What if you sincerely believe that blowing up infidels will give you a place in paradise? It does matter what you believe. Sincerity is never good enough, because you can be sincerely wrong, and you cannot afford to be wrong about Jesus.

The Jews had zeal, but it was misdirected, because they were trying to establish their own righteousness. They had a 'DIY' (do-it-yourself) religion. Why do people make that mistake? The root cause is pride. It is said that George Bernard Shaw once attended an Easter Mission in Cambridge, and as the speaker explained the substitutionary death of Jesus on the cross for sinners, he interrupted, *'I'll carry my own sins, thank you very much.'* What a fatal mistake, and what a fearful prospect, having to carry your own sins and come face to face with the holy God!

They had a word from God, but they complicated it
The third reason for Jewish unbelief is found in verses 5-13: they had a word from God, but they complicated it. Here Paul is quoting Moses' last sermon, recorded in Deuteronomy 30, where he sums up everything he has said to them. Moses puts himself into this sermon; he preaches to them as a dying man to dying men. You may well have books on your shelves explaining the Christian faith – *Basic Christianity* by John Stott, for example, or *Mere Christianity* by C. S. Lewis, or *Christianity Explored* by Rico Tice. Well, says Paul, here is another one by Moses: *The Way of Salvation Simply Explained.* 'Don't go the way of trying to establish your own righteousness,' says Moses; 'that is a dead end.' Describing the righteousness that is by the law, Moses says, *'The man who does these things will live by them'* (verse 5). But the point is this: Who can do these things?

That is what Jesus wanted the rich young ruler to understand. He claimed to have kept all the commandments since he was a youth (Luke 18). But when Jesus told him to 'Go, sell all you have and give to the poor', he couldn't do it. Keeping the Law is a dead end. To try and establish your own righteousness is the wrong way, says Moses, but he spells out the right way in the verses that follow:

> 'Do not say in your heart, "Who will ascend into heaven?" (that is, to bring Christ down) or "Who will descend into the deep?" (that is, to bring Christ up from the dead). But what does it say? "The word is near you; it is in your mouth and in your heart" that is, the word of faith we are proclaiming.'
>
> (Romans 10:6-8)

A story is told of Toscanini, the great conductor of the Philadelphia Philharmonic Orchestra. He was well known as a master of the art of negative motivation, and in his quest for perfection he would often berate and belittle his musicians. One night, after an almost flawless performance of Beethoven's Fifth Symphony, an enraptured audience applauded endlessly. When the plaudits were finally over, he turned restlessly to the orchestra and hoarsely whispered, 'Ladies and gentlemen, you are nothing, and I am nothing; but Beethoven – Beethoven is everything!'

It is not about your performance; it is about God's provision in Christ. You do not have to climb up into heaven, says Moses, because God has sent his Son down from heaven: 'Without ceasing to be what he eternally was, he became what he eternally was not.' The Word that was 'in the beginning with God [face to face with God]

. . . the Word became flesh and dwelt among us, and we beheld his glory . . . full of grace and truth' (John 1:2,14). Tell me this: if you can reach heaven under your own steam, why did he need to come down from heaven?

Neither do you have to go down into the depths to claw your way up out of the mess that you have got yourself into, because Christ has been there too. Crucified, dead and buried, he descended into hell. And on the third day God raised him from the dead. If you can atone for your own sins, why did Jesus need to descend into hell on the cross? All that is needed God has provided. All you need to do is believe in the Lord Jesus Christ. You just have to agree with God: God raised him from the dead; God vindicated him; God accepted his sacrifice; God exalted him. If you believe that in your heart, why not confess it with your mouth? That is the way of salvation. Don't complicate what God has made simple.

Ah, you say, but surely God helps those who help themselves? No, God helps those who cannot help themselves. But surely I need to clean up my life a little, to make some sort of improvement? No, you do not! But there is so much in my life I need to sort out first. No, there is not; it is salvation we are talking about, not self-help. But I need to sort out my theology and do a bit more thinking. No, you are not saved by correct theology; the living Christ saves you. Let him sort your theology out for you; let him become your teacher, your prophet. Ah, you say, maybe that is how you start, but surely it gets a bit more complicated afterwards? No, you go on as you came in.

When Paul opens his letter to the church in Corinth, he describes Christians as *all those everywhere who call on the name of our Lord Jesus Christ* (1 Corinthians 1:2). That is the whole Christian life. It is to call on the name of the Lord. You do not ever stop doing that. *Everyone who calls on the name of the Lord will be saved* (Romans 10:13).

A young friend of mine was a drug user and became a drug dealer. He spent some time in prison, and he lived in a weird house where they had all sorts of occult experiences. He is now in his early 30s and has a remarkable testimony. As he drove home one night, the devil was whispering in his ear, *'This is your last night on earth; you are going to die tonight.'* He felt his body shutting down and had to pull over to the side of the road. This young man had no church background whatsoever, but he just cried out, *'God, spare me! Let me at least go home to see my family before I die.'* And God heard!

Let me tell you about another man. He worked for many years in a barber's shop. A customer who used to witness to him enquired about his absence and was told that he was very ill. One day, while walking from the shop, this customer saw the man sitting in his car and approached him. As he wound down the car window, he said to him, *'I've been worried about you. Where have you been?'* *'Do you know,'* the man replied, *'I've kicked him in the face for forty years, and the moment I call on him he comes!'* The man was converted! He had blasphemed, hated Christ and ridiculed Christians all his life, and yet in his hour of need, the moment he called, Jesus was there! He is a very present help in trouble.

Are you addicted to some destructive pattern of living? Do you not want to be set free? You cannot free yourself; you are caught in the spider's web of sin; but you can call on the name of the Lord.

He breaks the power of cancelled sin,
He sets the prisoner free.
Charles Wesley (1707-88)

Are you an angry person, 'losing it' with your family, under great pressure at work? Are you scared or anxious? Are you despairing? Just call on the name of the Lord. It is not complicated. You do not have to go on a pilgrimage to Rome, or on the hajj to Mecca. Augustine said that he is *'nearer than breath and breathing'.* If you need rescuing, then just cry, *'Lord, help me!'* Call on the name of the Lord and you will be saved.

On one occasion, when Abraham Lincoln had to sign some momentous document that had great consequences, he spent a whole night pacing the floor of his study. But In the end, of course, all he had to do was put his signature to it. To sign that document, to call on Jesus, is a very simple thing to do: *'The word is in your mouth',* on the tip of your tongue. But, of course, calling him into your life as your Lord and Saviour will have momentous consequences for you.

In Romans chapter 9, nobody becomes a Christian unless God calls them. In Romans chapter 10, anyone who calls on the name of the Lord will be saved; in fact, everyone who does so will be saved – not 'may be', but 'will be'. If it is really that simple, then why do the Jews not believe? They have a foundation, but they have stumbled over it; they have zeal, but it is misdirected; they have the way of salvation simply explained to them, but they have complicated it.

They have messengers sent to them
The last reason Paul gives is that they have messengers sent to them. Have you noticed in these chapters the number of quotations from the Old Testament? Here in Romans 10:14-21 we have a cluster of them. It is not as if the Jews have not heard, for God has sent his messengers to them time and time again; but they have refused to listen. They have behaved as children do when they do not want to hear: they keep stuffing their fingers in their ears and talking about something else.

Why do people not believe? Is it because they have not heard? The red herring so often thrown in when you are trying to talk to someone about Jesus is, *'But what about those who haven't heard?'* In answer to that question Paul would say, *'Well now, I don't know who you are talking about. Who are these people?'* He quotes from Psalm 19: *'Did they not hear? Of course they did*: "*Their voice has gone out into all the earth, their words to the ends of the world"'* (Romans 10:18). The point he is making is quite simply this: in the first half of Psalm 19 the psalmist speaks about the testimony of the creation to its Creator and asserts that no one can say that they have not heard. Paul makes the same point in Romans chapter 1: *'What may be known about God is plain to them . . . For since the creation of the world God's invisible qualities – his eternal power and divine nature – have been clearly seen . . . so that men are without excuse'* (Romans 1:19-20).

The problem, he says, is not that they have not heard and do not know the truth, but that they have suppressed the truth (Romans 1:18).

Many years ago in *The Monthly Record* Donald MacLeod wrote:

> *'Man is so made that he cannot but infer from his environment the eternal power of the Godhead of God. [The God-ness of God, you might say.] Man's mind, indeed his whole psychology, is tuned in to the revelation which surrounds him. And this is as true today as it has ever been. A generation that can peer into the structure of the atom and stand on the surface of the moon has more reason to believe in God, not less.'*

It is not that they have not heard. Every moment of every day the message goes out:

> *'Jesus is Lord!' Creation's voice proclaims it.*
> *For by His power each tree and flower*
> *Was planned and made,*
> *'Jesus is Lord!' the universe declares it,*
> *Sun, moon and stars in heaven cry,*
> *'Jesus is Lord!'*
>   David J. Mansell (b. 1936)

But there is more to it than that. Psalm 19 goes on to speak of the law of the Lord, which converts the heart. God's voice in creation leaves us without excuse, but it does not convert us. What about the message of salvation in Christ? Well, says Paul, that message also has gone out around the world. *'From Jerusalem all the way around to Illyricum* [that is, modern-day Albania] *I have fully proclaimed the gospel of Christ'* (Romans 15:19).

Paul's answer to the question, *'What about those who have not heard?'* is, *'Well, let us make sure that they do hear.'* Election and evangelism go hand in hand. Romans chapters 9 and 10 belong together. God chooses people, but how do they come to believe in Jesus?

> *'How, then, can they call on the one they have not believed in? And how can they believe in the one of whom they have not heard? And how can they hear without someone preaching to them? And how can they preach unless they are sent?'*
> (Romans 10:14-15)

The reason people believe and trust in Jesus is because they have had something explained to them; they have heard the message. And the reason they have heard the message is because someone has come to preach and explain it to them. Is it not true that the only reason you and I know this message is because someone has bothered to do that for us? Someone took the trouble to put on their shoes, get off their couches, book tickets and board aeroplanes, often at great personal cost to themselves and their families. So many of those pioneer missionaries packed up all their earthly belongings into a coffin. They did not need a suitcase because they were not coming back; they were going to a place where they would almost certainly die, but they went nevertheless because they had this message that people needed to hear. *'How beautiful are the feet of those who bring good news!'* (Romans 10:15).

Geraint Fielder in *Life Lines* tells the moving story of how the Bible came to Korea. In 1863 Robert Thomas, from the village of Llanover near Abergavenny, set sail for China with his young wife. She and their child died in Shanghai just months after they arrived. While in China he met some Koreans and began to learn the Korean language. As the only known European in China able to speak Korean, it was decided to put him on an American trading ship as an interpreter. His motive was purely to bring Bibles to Korea, and as the ship sailed up the river to Pyongyang, Robert Thomas began to throw Bibles ashore. But the Korean Government, fearing Western imperialism, saw the ship's advance as a threat, so when it became stranded on mud flats it was set alight. Thomas waded ashore in the shallow water, taking his Bibles with him, but as the people from the ship landed, every one of them was executed.

What became of those Bibles? A Korean who later became a Christian said that his father had picked up one of them, and that children took Bibles home, and their parents used them for wallpaper. Then people started to read their wallpaper, and the message of God's love for the world, which had been silenced on Thomas's lips, changed their lives. Others believed too, so that when American missionaries arrived there twenty years later, they found a dozen or more Koreans who shared the same faith as Robert Thomas. Thomas himself had died, but churches sprang up. Beautiful feet that had only left their footprint in the mud, but the Word of God took root and transformed a nation! In South Korea today, one in four people are Bible-believing Christians, and they are sending missionaries all over the world.

Do you have beautiful feet? Faith comes by hearing the Word of Christ. Hearing comes by preaching. Preaching comes when Christians get off their couches, put on their gospel boots and go and tell people about Jesus.

What happens when Christians do that? God stretches out his arms to the lost. I love the body language in verse 21. Has God finished with the Jews? Does he fold his arms and turn his back upon them? No! *'All day long I have held out my hands to a disobedient and obstinate people.'* That is the way we are to share the gospel with others: not with arms folded and fingers wagging, not tongue in cheek ('I wonder if they are one of the elect'), but freely offering this gospel to all indiscriminately, with arms outstretched, welcoming people to Jesus. And as we do that, something else happens. In most translations, verse 14b reads as in the NIV: *'And how can they believe in the one of whom they have not heard?'*, but the better translation is: *'How can they believe in the one they have not heard?'* (ESV's marginal alternative). What a high view of preaching that is! One of the old Puritans put it like this: *'Christ comes to the people in the chariot of the preached word.'* This is what preaching is about: Christ coming to us. As Paul said to the Ephesians, this Christ, who has broken down the middle wall of partition between Jew and Gentile and made peace through his death on the cross – *'He came and preached peace to you who were far away'* – you Gentiles in Ephesus (Ephesians 2:14-18). When did Jesus ever set foot in Ephesus?

He came to them through the Spirit-anointed gospel preaching of the apostle Paul. Let us never for one moment think that we can replace preaching. How will people believe, if they do not hear him speaking to them and calling them through the preaching of the word?

So do not be a chapter 9 Christian or a chapter 10 Christian. Be a chapter 9 and a chapter 10 Christian, thoroughly convinced that God sovereignly chooses and calls people to himself, and utterly persuaded that he does so as people such as you and I obediently go out at the call of God to preach to those who do not know him.

Are you wondering today if you have beautiful feet? Is God calling you to be a missionary? He almost certainly is. As far as Paul is concerned, you are either a missionary or you are the mission field.

Chapter 3
The mystery of Israel
Romans 11

Chapters 9–11 of Romans deal with one of the greatest turnabouts in the history of the world. With the coming of Jesus, the Gentiles, whose lives have been going in a wrong direction away from God, are suddenly at the centre of the Messiah's kingdom, while the Jews, whose whole orientation has been towards God and towards righteousness, in a weird reversal of fortunes find themselves on the outside. It is like the parable of the two sons in Luke 15: the runaway son comes home and the party is held for him, but the dutiful, stay-at-home son stands outside, angry and left in the cold.

A personal concern

Paul is troubled by this turn of events, and in these chapters he is trying to work out how and why it has happened. For him, it is not just an academic exercise, it is personal: *'I am an Israelite myself, a descendant of Abraham, from the tribe of Benjamin'* (Romans 11:1). This situation is breaking his heart, causing *'great sorrow and unceasing anguish'* (9:2). It drives him to his knees in *'prayer to God for the Israelites . . . that they may be saved'* (10:1). It dictates his evangelistic strategy, forcing him to go time and time again to the Jew first, even though they keep slamming the door in his face.

In 1 Corinthians 9:20 Paul says, '*To the Jews, I became like a Jew, to win the Jews.*' But Paul was a Jew, so what does he mean? In 2 Corinthians 11, amidst a catalogue of his sufferings for the sake of Christ and the gospel, he says, '*Five times I received from the Jews the forty lashes minus one.*' This punishment of thirty-nine lashes was one that, under the Roman Empire, the Jews were allowed to administer for certain offences. On five occasions, then, Paul had been flogged by the Jews to within an inch of his life. Yet Paul was also a Roman citizen, so why did he not avoid this punishment by calling on his Roman citizenship? Surely it was because he did not want anything to interfere with his desire to win Jews for Jesus.

A pastoral concern

This turn of events was of concern to Paul not only personally, but also pastorally. In Romans 11:13 he says, '*Now I am speaking to you Gentiles. Inasmuch then as I am an apostle to the Gentiles . . .*' The church in Rome to which he was writing was in all probability planted by Jewish people who had come from Rome to Jerusalem for the feast and were in the crowd on the day of Pentecost when three thousand were converted. They may have still been there when a further five thousand were added to the church, but after their time in Jerusalem they would have dispersed again to the distant points of the Empire. So, initially, the church in Rome would have consisted mainly – probably almost entirely – of Jewish believers.

But then in AD 48, when Claudius kicked the Jews out of Rome, the church would have become largely a Gentile church. In view of the culture clash indicated in

Romans 14, there may well have been some Jews among them at the time Paul was writing, but at this point in his letter he is concerned to speak particularly to the Gentiles: *'Don't forget this, you Gentiles! Claudius may have kicked the Jews out of Rome, but don't you dare kick them out of your church! When God is stretching out his arms to a disobedient and rebellious people, don't you turn your back upon them!'* Reading between the lines, it seems to me that Paul is warning Gentile Christians against arrogance and superiority and, worse than that, anti-Semitism. Later on he says:

> *'May the God who gives endurance and encouragement give you a spirit of unity among yourselves as you follow Christ Jesus, so that with one heart and mouth* [Jew and Gentile together] *you may glorify the God and Father of our Lord Jesus Christ. Accept one another, then, just as Christ accepted you, in order to bring praise to God. For I tell you that Christ has become a servant of the Jews on behalf of God's truth, to confirm the promises made to the patriarchs so that the Gentiles may glorify God for his mercy . . .'*

> (Romans 15:5-9)

A theological concern

Paul's concern in relation to this turnabout is also theological:

> *'As far as the gospel is concerned, they* [the Jews] *are enemies on your account; but as far as election is concerned, they are loved on account*

of the patriarchs, for God's gifts and his call are irrevocable. Just as you who were at one time disobedient to God have now received mercy as a result of their disobedience, so they too have now become disobedient in order that they too may now receive mercy as a result of God's mercy to you. For God has bound all men over to disobedience so that he may have mercy on them all.'

(Romans 11:28-32)

At the moment, the Jewish people may be opposing and persecuting Christians and throwing them out of their synagogues, but God's covenant and promise are irrevocable. God entered into an eternal covenant with Abraham. Has he welched on that deal, or does Israel have a future in the plans and purposes of God? That is what this chapter is about: it is not just the history of Israel, but the mystery of Israel:

'I do not want you to be ignorant of this mystery, brothers, so that you may not be conceited: Israel has experienced a hardening in part until the full number of the Gentiles has come in. And so all Israel will be saved . . .'

(Romans 11:25-26)

What Paul is saying is that there is a huge secret in the Bible that he wants to share with us. The word he uses for it is 'mystery', a technical term that simply means something that God has revealed – something we would never have guessed unless God had told us. Look at the very end of Romans:

The mystery of Israel

'Now to him who is able to establish you by my gospel and the proclamation of Jesus Christ, according to the revelation of the mystery hidden for long ages past, but now revealed and made known through the prophetic writings by the command of the eternal God, so that all nations might believe and obey him – to the only wise God be glory for ever through Jesus Christ! Amen.'
(Romans 16:25-27)

The word 'mystery' is another word for the gospel. The gospel is an open secret, and it concerns the Jews. Has God finished with the Jewish people? Paul's response to this question is an emphatic negative: *'Did God reject his people? By no means!'* (Romans 11:1); *'Did they stumble so as to fall beyond recovery? Not at all!'* (11:11). Israel has a past; Israel has a present; Israel has a future. Her past rejection of her Messiah does not mean that God has written her off. That idea has been at the root of so much anti-Semitism in the Christian Church. But the fact that the Jews rejected their Messiah does not mean that God has turned his back on them. Israel's present unbelief is not total; it is not pointless, and it is not final.

Israel's fall is not total (verses 1-10)
First, he argues, Israel's fall is not total. Paul himself is proof of this fact: *'I am an Israelite myself, a descendant of Abraham, from the tribe of Benjamin'* (verse 1). *'God didn't reject his people,'* he is saying; *'God didn't reject me. If ever a Jew deserved to be tossed out for rejecting the Messiah, it's me.'* Listen to his testimony elsewhere:

'Even though I was once a blasphemer and a persecutor and a violent man, I was shown mercy because I acted in ignorance and unbelief. The grace of our Lord was poured out on me abundantly, along with the faith and love that are in Christ Jesus. Here is a trustworthy saying that deserves full acceptance: Christ Jesus came into the world to save sinners – of whom I am the worst. But for that very reason I was shown mercy so that in me, the worst of sinners, Christ Jesus might display his unlimited patience as an example to those who would believe on him and receive eternal life. [Then he bursts into praise.] *Now to the King eternal, immortal, invisible, the only God, be honour and glory for ever and ever. Amen.'*

(1 Timothy 1:12-17)

'If God can save me,' says Paul, *'he can save anybody.'* Spurgeon puts it like this:

'If a bridge is strong enough to bear an elephant, it will most certainly carry a mouse; and if the greatest sinner who ever lived has entered heaven by the bridge of the atoning sacrifice of Christ, then no one who has ever lived can say, 'My sin is beyond forgiveness.''

So never write anyone off, however hard the case may seem. Why did Paul keep knocking on synagogue doors? Why did he keep exposing himself to such threats and persecution? Why did he become as a Jew to win the Jews? Because of what God had done in his life. If you want any justification for Jewish evangelism, Paul says, look at what God has done to me! What a wonderful argument that is! Perhaps when you look at your family circle or amongst your friends, you lose hope that that person you have been praying for will ever be saved. Well, just think what God has done in your life! If he can do it for you, he can do it for anyone, can't he?

Maybe you have heard of the Starfish Foundation, an international development charity working with Aids in South Africa. Someone was watching a man standing on a beach where thousands of starfish had been thrown up by the tide; the man was picking the starfish up one by one and throwing them back into the sea. *'What are you doing that for?'* asked the onlooker. *'I'm saving the starfish,'* he said. *'But there are thousands of them: what difference can it make just to throw a few back into the sea?'* Throwing back one more, he replied, *'It made a difference to that one.'* So the Starfish Foundation was started, to tackle the problem of Aids in South Africa, one at a time. Has God finished with the Jewish people? *'No,'* says Paul, *'I'm a Jew, and God saved me. It made a difference to this one.'*

But it is not just a case of the occasional conversion from amongst the Jewish people; it is bigger than that; there is a remnant.

> *'Don't you know what the Scripture says in the passage about Elijah – how he appealed to God against Israel: "Lord, they have killed your prophets and torn down your altars; I am the only one left, and they are trying to kill me"? And*

what was God's answer to him? "I have reserved
for myself seven thousand who have not bowed
the knee to Baal" So too, at the present time,
there is a remnant chosen by grace.'

(Romans 11:2-4)

The time of Elijah must have been Israel's darkest hour. Things were so far gone under Ahab and Jezebel that Elijah actually pleaded with God against Israel. He is using here a technical term from the law courts – bringing a lawsuit against them, lodging an official complaint. Back in Genesis 18, we find Abraham pleading with God on behalf of the pagan city of Sodom, but here is Elijah pleading with God against Israel! Israel, Elijah thought, had fallen beyond any hope of recovery, and God must have finished with them. But what does God say? *'I have reserved for myself seven thousand who have not bowed the knee to Baal.'*

Dale Ralph Davis, in his commentary on 1 Kings, says, *'It is the Old Testament equivalent of Jesus saying, "I will build my church and the gates of hell will not prevail against it (Matthew 16:18)".* One of those seven thousand was Obadiah – and there he was in Ahab's administration, right under Ahab's nose! Even in the worst of times, when it looks like wholesale apostasy, God never leaves himself without a witness. There is always 'a remnant according to the election of grace', and it is much bigger than you think.

When Paul went up to Jerusalem with 'the collection' from Gentile Christians to relieve famine and persecution amongst Jewish Christians in Jerusalem,

Luke tells us:

> 'When we arrived at Jerusalem the brothers
> received us warmly. The next day Paul and the
> rest of us went to see James, and all the elders
> were present. Paul greeted them and reported
> in detail what God had been doing among the
> Gentiles through his ministry. When they heard
> this, they praised God. Then they said to Paul:
> "You see, brother, how many thousands of Jews
> have believed . . ."'
>
> (Acts 21:17-21)

There were Jewish believers, thousands of them!
Indeed, someone has estimated that, when Paul wrote
Romans, there may well have been upward of three
hundred thousand Jewish believers in the Christian
church. So Israel's fall is not total.

Israel's fall is not pointless (verses 11-24)
Secondly, Israel's fall is not pointless. It was all part of
the plan and purpose of God to save the world, and
to fulfil his promise to Abraham to bring the blessing
of Abraham to all the nations. *Again I ask: Did they
stumble so as to fall beyond recovery? Not at all! Rather,
because of their transgression, salvation has come to the
Gentiles to make Israel envious'* (Romans 11:11).

No wonder Paul calls Israel's reversal of fortune a
mystery! If you had to come up with a plan to save the
world, you would never have come up with a plan like
that. No wonder he bursts into praise at the end of this
chapter:

'Oh, the depth of the riches of the wisdom and knowledge of God! How unsearchable his judgments, and his paths beyond tracing out. Who has known the mind of the Lord? Or who has been his counsellor? . . . For from him and through him and to him are all things. To him be the glory for ever! Amen.'

(Romans 11:33-36)

Paul uses a horticultural metaphor to try and explain to us what is happening. He talks about the olive tree, which is a biblical symbol of Israel (Jeremiah 11:16). God has not uprooted the olive tree; he has only broken off some branches. He has broken off some dead wood in order to bring in Gentiles, so that we might be nurtured by the same root, so that the Jewish Scriptures might also become our Scriptures, and so that we might call Yahweh 'Abba'!

'Consider, therefore,' he says, *'the kindness and sternness of God: sternness to those who fell, but kindness to you, provided that you continue in his kindness. Otherwise you also will be cut off'* (11:22). Think about that – the kindness and the sternness of God. The Bible does not teach that God hates the sin but loves the sinner; it says that he is angry with the sinner every day. But, unlike our anger, his anger is that of a loving God; he is angrily loving and lovingly angry. The amazing thing is that when God gets angry he reaches out to people. No wonder Paul bursts into song!

Something very scary and yet at the same time very wonderful is happening here. God has not uprooted the olive tree; he has broken off the dead wood so that he can graft you in. But don't become proud, Paul says to the church in Rome. The only reason that you are Christians at all is because of the kindness and sternness of God, in his desire to save his ancient people:

> '. . . because of their transgression, salvation has come to the Gentiles to make Israel envious. But if their transgression means riches for the world, and their loss means riches for the Gentiles, how much greater riches will their fulness bring!'
>
> (Romans 11:11-12)

What God wants is more than a remnant. Think again of the parable of the two sons in Luke 15. Both sons are lost, one far away, the other close to home. At the end of the parable the older brother, who had stayed dutifully at home, became angry at seeing grace lavished upon his younger brother and refused to come in to the party. So his father went out and pleaded with him. That is what God is doing in the world today. As Gentiles are being brought in, God is pleading with the older brother, provoking him to jealousy, and longing for him to come in.

Now, while not strictly parallel in terms of salvation history, we can see a similar dynamic at work today. The focal point of Christianity now is not in Wales, Britain, Europe or America; it has shifted to Africa, Latin America and Asia, and in all these countries people are coming in their hundreds and thousands to faith in Jesus Christ. How do we react? Do we sit back and sulk, like the older brother in the parable, pining for the good old days? In former days, God in his grace and kindness sent revival after revival to Wales; but that is in the past, and we have no divine right to expect him to do it again. What if, instead of feeling sorry for ourselves, we were to feel challenged by what God is doing elsewhere in the world, and stirred up with godly envy and a longing that he would do a new work amongst us? That is the kind of dynamic Paul is describing here. I love Eugene Peterson's paraphrase of verses 11 and 12:

> *'When [the Jews] walked out, they left the door open and the outsiders walked in. But the next thing you know, the Jews were starting to wonder if perhaps they had walked out on a good thing. Now, if their leaving triggered this worldwide coming of non-Jewish outsiders to God's kingdom, just imagine the effect of their coming back! What a homecoming!'*

God is working out his plans and purposes. He has not moved on to Plan B; he is sovereignly carrying out his purposes, and he knows what he is doing.

Israel's fall is not final (verses 25-32)
Israel's fall is not total, nor is it pointless and, lastly, it is not final. The remnant are not 'leftovers'. They are described in verse 16 as the 'firstfruits', the promise of a spiritual harvest among the Jews. Such an outcome is more than hinted at in these verses:

> *'But if their transgression means riches for the world, and their loss means riches for the*

> *Gentiles, how much greater riches will their*
> *fulness bring! . . . For if their rejection is the*
> *reconciliation of the world, what will their*
> *acceptance be but life from the dead?'*
>
> (Romans 11:12, 15)

Commenting on this, Matthew Henry says:

> *'If the putting out of their candle was the*
> *lighting of yours, by that power of God, who*
> *brings good out of evil; much more shall the*
> *continued light of your candle, when God's time*
> *is come, be a means of lighting theirs again.'*

And the repercussions of that, says Paul, will be immense – the expression he uses is 'life from the dead'. By this, Paul does not mean the resurrection; he would have used the word *anastasis* for that, as he did when he talked about wanting to *'attain to the resurrection from the dead'* (Philippians 3:11). I believe he is talking here about Ezekiel's vision of the valley of dry bones (Ezekiel 37). Try to imagine Paul's experience as he went around the Mediterranean, fronting up to the synagogues Sabbath after Sabbath! He must surely have asked himself at times, *'Can these bones live?'*

Let us be clear that we are not talking about anything political. What we have here is to be understood spiritually and evangelistically: it is to be understood in terms of revival, the spiritual restoration of the kingdom of Israel – such a widespread revival amongst Jewish people that *'all Israel will be saved'* (verse 26).

What does 'all Israel' mean?

Some say that 'all Israel' means the Church, made up of Jews and Gentiles. But that would be very confusing, because in these three chapters Paul has talked about 'Israel' eleven times, and each time he is referring to his fellow Jews. In verse 25 he says, '*I do not want you to be ignorant of this mystery, brothers, so that you may not be conceited: Israel has experienced a hardening in part until the full number of the Gentiles has come in.*' So it would be very confusing if suddenly, in mid-sentence and mid-argument, Paul started to use the word 'Israel' to mean the 'new Israel' or the 'true Israel.'

Others say that Paul is talking about the elect Jews, the Israel within Israel. But if Paul is simply saying that all the elect Jews will be saved, then that is hardly a 'mystery.' What, then, does he mean?

In 2 Corinthians 3:14-16, Paul talks about the veil being taken away:

> '*But their minds were made dull, for to this day the same veil remains when the old covenant is read. It has not been removed, because only in Christ is it taken away. Even to this day when Moses is read, a veil covers their hearts. But whenever anyone turns to the Lord, the veil is taken away.*'

What is being promised is a 'turning to the Lord' on an unprecedented scale. Somewhere, at some time, God is going to lift the veil that prevents Israel from seeing the truth of the gospel, and there will be such a widespread turning to the Lord that you will be able to say that 'all Israel' is saved. That is not the same as saying that every Jew will be saved. If you say, for example, '*They are all Welsh in Aberystwyth*,' you do not mean that every single person is Welsh; it just seems like that. In the same way, there will come a time when 'all Israel' will be worshipping the Lamb of God: not 'every Israelite', but 'all Israel'. Thomas Goodwin put it like this:

> '*There will come a time when the generality of mankind, both Jew and Gentile, will come to Jesus Christ. He hath had but little takings of the world yet, but he will have before he hath done.*'

That is God's intention: overflowing grace, spilling over freely from one to another. And that is what he is doing in the world now, so that all nations, tribes and tongues will be there around the throne – and amongst them the Jewish nation and the Hebrew tongue.

Our response
How does this 'mystery' apply to us, and what impact should it have?

It ought to humble us
The reason Paul wrote to a predominantly Gentile Church in Rome about the future of the Jews was to put the Gentiles in their place. '*Do not be arrogant, but be afraid*,' he says (verse 20); '*do not boast*' (verse 18); '*do not be conceited*' (verse 25). There is no place for pride or arrogance or anti-Semitism. We Gentiles are guests in Israel's house

It ought to excite us

Such a hope ought to excite us. *The Westminster Larger Catechism* says that when we pray the second petition of the Lord's Prayer ('Your kingdom come . . .')

> 'We pray, that the kingdom of sin and Satan may be destroyed, the gospel propagated throughout the world, the Jews called, the fullness of the Gentiles brought in . . . that Christ would rule in our hearts here, and hasten the time of his second coming . . .'

In the eighteenth century, this hope drove men and women around the world to start 'concerts of prayer' and launched the modern missions movement.

A. W. Pink said, *'Hope does not hold up the head of our holy desires.'* Though we may have holy desires, if they are not upheld by hope, we resign ourselves to just another day of small things and we expect the faith to dwindle away to nothing. In his exposition of Psalm 86:9, Charles Spurgeon wrote:

> 'David was not a believer in the theory that the world will grow worse and worse, and that the dispensation will wind up with general darkness, and idolatry. Earth's sun is to go down amid tenfold night if some of our prophetic brethren are to be believed. Not so do we expect, but we look for a day, when the dwellers in all lands shall learn righteousness, shall trust in the Saviour, shall worship thee alone, O God, "and shall glorify thy name". The modern notion has greatly damped

the zeal of the church for missions, and the sooner it is shown to be unscriptural the better it will be for the cause of God. It neither consorts with prophecy, honours God, nor inspires the Church with ardour. Far hence be it driven.'

This great hope should 'hold up the head of our holy desires' and make us confident in the certain success of the gospel. It should excite us to pray and to work together. Let us agree to disagree on minor things, while respecting one another's convictions, and let us get on with the real business of preaching the gospel, which Jesus said must be preached to all the nations before the end will come.

It ought to lead us to worship

At the end of this chapter, theology becomes doxology as Paul bursts into a song of praise and worship. Our God is not some tribal deity. He is the God of the world, the sovereign Lord of human history.

'Oh, the depth of the riches of the wisdom and knowledge of God! How unsearchable his judgments, and his paths beyond tracing out! Who has known the mind of the Lord, or who has been his counsellor? Who has ever given to God, that God should repay him? For from him and through him and to him are all things. To him be the glory for ever! Amen.'

(Romans 11:33-36)

Chapter 4
'To boldly go where no one has been before'
Romans 15:14-33

'It has always been my ambition,' says Paul, *'to preach the gospel where Christ was not known'* (Romans 15:20). I think it was Francis Xavier, founder of the Jesuits in the seventeenth century, who famously challenged a bunch of university students in his day to *'Give up your small ambitions; come with me and save the world.'* That is what Paul wants to say to the church in Rome. His letter to them is not a systematic theology for Bible nerds; it is an apology for worldwide evangelisation from the apostle to the Gentiles. And if you do not find that the effect of reading Romans, or studying it in Bible study groups, or preaching through it, is to make you and your people want to share the gospel, especially with those who have never heard it before, then you have missed the whole point. It is a sad commentary on today's church that those of us who call ourselves evangelicals are often not evangelistic, and those who are evangelistic are often not evangelical. Such a situation would never have met with Paul's approval. James Denney once said: *'The Church is healthiest when its evangelists are theologians, and its theologians are evangelists.'* I believe that is why Paul wrote Romans: to establish Christians at the heart of the

Empire in his gospel, so that they would embrace that gospel with him and send him out with it to the Western world.

Someone has said that in most churches and denominations today, mission comes very low on the agenda – under 'Any other business' rather than 'Matters arising'. Indeed, if we are honest, it doesn't even come up under 'Apologies for absence' in some churches. Paul's concern in writing this letter is that the Roman church should put God's mission to the world on their agenda. I hope we are by now familiar with the idea that every member is a minister, in keeping with the biblical teaching on the priesthood of all believers; but we need also to recognise that every member is a missionary. Whatever gifts God has given us as a congregation, we are partnering together to get the gospel out into the world. That is what the church is, and that is what Israel was supposed to be – God's missionary task force, on mission, together with God, bringing the gospel to the world.

If God's people are sharing together in God's mission to the world, what will this look like?

Proclaiming Christ
First and foremost, mission is proclaiming Christ. This comes out very clearly in Paul's words: *from Jerusalem all the way round to Illyricum I have fully proclaimed the gospel of Christ'* (verse 19). I heard recently of two ministers who were turned down by a particular missionary society because they were only Bible teachers; since they had no other skills, the society could

not place them. Granted, there are problems of access into some countries, but we must never forget that mission is essentially proclaiming Christ.

The language Paul uses to describe this activity is not what we might expect:

> *'I have written to you . . . because of the grace God gave me to be a minister of Christ Jesus to the Gentiles with the priestly duty of proclaiming the gospel of God, so that the Gentiles might become an offering acceptable to God, sanctified by the Holy Spirit.'*
>
> (Romans 15:15-16)

This is the language of Old Testament worship; it is temple terminology. The word Paul uses for 'minister' translates literally as 'liturgist' – he is a "liturgist" of Christ Jesus to the Gentiles'.

Is that the way you see evangelism? Have you ever thought of missionary work as worship? People sometimes drive a wedge between evangelism and worship, but according to Paul here, evangelism is worship. To him, proclaiming the gospel of God to the Gentiles is his priestly duty, and those who are converted under his ministry are an offering he is bringing to God. They have been set apart by the Holy Spirit under his preaching, and he brings them to God as an offering of worship.

Priestly ministry is not offering a sacrifice at an altar; it is proclaiming Christ. When Paul writes to the Corinthians about the Lord's Supper, he says, *'whenever you eat this bread and drink this cup, you proclaim the Lord's death'* (1 Corinthians 11:26). The Lord's Supper is a visible gospel sermon. It is not about a priest standing at the altar to re-present Christ to God, as Roman Catholics believe. It is about representing Christ, not re-presenting him. We go to the world, not with bread and wine, but with the message of the finished work of Christ on the cross. As Luther put it, *'We live as though Christ died yesterday, rose again today, and is coming back tomorrow.'* That is what the Lord's Supper is all about, and that is our message: the good news of the once-and-for-all sacrifice of Jesus on the cross, by which the middle wall of partition has come down, so that now in Christ there is neither Jew nor Gentile, but all are one in Christ Jesus.

The Collection

In the ancient world, the Jew–Gentile divide was huge, and yet in Christ and through the proclamation of the gospel that wall has come down. The proof of that is 'the Collection' (verse 26). It is a powerful demonstration of God's grace. While Paul has been travelling around the eastern Mediterranean, planting churches, he has also been taking up a collection, an offering from the Gentiles for Jewish believers in Jerusalem who are suffering from persecution and famine. He has reminded these Gentile churches of their indebtedness to the Jewish people:

'Macedonia and Achaia were pleased to make a contribution for the poor among the saints at Jerusalem . . . and indeed they owe it to them. For if the Gentiles have shared in the Jews' spiritual blessings, they owe it to the Jews to share with them their material blessings.'

(Romans 15:26-27)

We Gentiles have received so much from the Jews' treasure house. We have their Scriptures; we have their Messiah; we have their God as our God; we have the covenants and the promises – and to all these things we were once strangers! The 'collection' proves the power of God to reconcile people to himself and to each other.

A couple of years ago I attended a conference in Iowa, USA; it was concerned with church-based theological education for people involved in church-planting movements. The church is expanding rapidly in the global South, but it is very shallow. While there are many leaders and evangelists and preachers, they have no theological training and cannot go to a theological seminary. This movement is trying to provide quality theological training for such people, but without taking them out of their situations and interrupting their ministry. Among those who attended were two men from the Congo, joint leaders of a church-planting movement consisting of about seven thousand churches. They had been on opposite sides of a civil war; in fact, one had been personally responsible for the massacre of the other's family; but they were in this conference as brothers in the Lord and fellow labourers. That is what the gospel does!

And that is what the gospel had been doing all over the eastern Mediterranean. From 'Jerusalem all the way to Illyricum', up to the shores of the Adriatic, reaching into Serbia, Albania and Macedonia, walls had been coming down and people had come out of their ghettoes and embraced one another in Christ.

When Paul says that he has *fully proclaimed the gospel of Christ* in those regions, he obviously does not mean every single person living there has been saved. His policy was to go to strategic population centres and plant churches. He planted a church in Ephesus, for example, and then that church planted churches in the Lycus valley. There were about eleven churches in that valley; amongst them, Laodicea and Colossae. And so it went on. He says of the church in Thessalonica: *'The Lord's message rang out from you not only in Macedonia and Achaia – your faith in God has become known everywhere'* (1 Thessalonians 1:8). Indeed he says of the church in Rome: *'I thank my God through Jesus Christ for all of you, because your faith is being reported all over the world'* (Romans 1:8). Imagine what these cities must have been like under the Roman Empire! There would have been people from Spain, Algeria, Libya, Egypt, Ethiopia, Somalia, Iran, Iraq, Turkey, Armenia, Ukraine and Saudi Arabia. They had contact with Russia, India, Thailand, Burma and the great civilisations of China. The streets of the Empire's cities were even walked by the descendants of a million slaves that Julius Caesar had brought home from a certain rough northern region with its warlike, primitive people, so those first Christians could well have met an ancient Briton! And as the gospel penetrated such diverse communities, people came together and sat around the Lord's Table, all one in Christ Jesus! This was reported all over the world.

Pioneering

Secondly, mission is pioneering. *'It has always been my ambition'*, says Paul, *'to preach the gospel where Christ was not known'* (Romans 15:20). Star Trek fans would say, *'to boldly go where no one has been before,'* and for them, of course, the final frontier is space. Back in 1768 there was a 39-year-old British sea captain who set off on a journey of scientific discovery. He had been hired by the Royal Society to observe the transit of Venus across the sun, and the journey would take him quite literally into uncharted waters. When eventually he saw a shoreline, it reminded him of South Wales, and so he called it New South Wales. Here is a line from Captain Cook's journal: *'I had ambition not only to go further than any man had been before, but as far as it was possible for man to go.'*

That was Paul's great ambition: *'to boldly go where no one had been before'* with the gospel! Not because he was an adventurer (though he may well have been), but because he had scriptural warrant for it. It is great to have ambition, but make sure your ambition rests on the foundation of Scripture! Paul's ambition came right out of the Scriptures: *'as it is written: "Those who were not told about him will see, and those who have not heard will understand"'* (Romans 15: 21). He is quoting here from Isaiah 52, one of the Servant Songs speaking about Jesus, the Suffering Servant. Jesus came as a missionary, and he wants his followers to be the same, *'to boldly go where no one has been before',* so that *'Those who were not told will see, and those who have not heard will understand.'*

When the London Missionary Society interviewed David Livingston, he was asked where he wanted to go. *'Anywhere as long as it's forward,'* he replied. When he arrived in Africa, he wrote home saying that he was *'haunted by the smoke of a thousand villages'* stretching out before him. All those communities where there was no gospel church; all those people who were without hope and without God in this world – these things haunted him and disturbed his sleep.

Now you might think that after so many centuries of missionary activity, no one really needs to pioneer today; there would be nowhere left for us to go with the gospel. Well, you would be totally wrong. The need is ten times greater today than it was in Paul's day: there are ten times as many unreached people in the world now as there were in Paul's day; eight million Muslims in Europe are unevangelised; one in five has never heard of Jesus; dozens and dozens of people groups are without a Bible in their own language, and there are whole nations without a church. That is the world we live in.

I remember reading a story of an African bishop who was being shown around a parish church somewhere in England. The vicar told him proudly, *'Our church has been here for eight hundred years preaching the gospel.'* The bishop responded, *'What took you so long?'* C. T. Studd once asked, *'Why should anyone have the opportunity to reject the gospel twice, when some have not had the opportunity to hear it once?'* Still today there are people waiting to hear for the first time – waiting for us to put on our gospel boots to go and tell them about Jesus. For *'how can they hear without someone preaching to them? And how can they preach unless they are sent?'*

Most of us spend most of our time with those who already know the gospel. That is an occupational hazard for ministers especially. I remember reading the story of a young pastor who one night received two phone calls, one after the other. Two men in his town were dying: one had been rushed to hospital on one side of town; the other was already in hospital thirty minutes in the other direction. One was an elder in the church, the other a God-denying man well-known in the community for his dislike of the church and everything it stood for. Both were calling for the pastor, and he had to decide which one to visit. What was he to do? Well, he prayed, of course, and then he hurried to the bedside of the unsaved sinner. As it turned out, the tough old sinner repented and put his trust in Jesus; he died a few years later, reconciled to God. The elder recovered but, furious because the pastor had not come immediately to visit him, he and his family left the church. *'To boldly go where no one has been before'* is not merely an academic question but one that confronts us every day – and not just those of us who are in the ministry.

In any community there are people who never darken the door of any church. Who are they? Who are the people we are not reaching, and where are they? I know of one church plant in Sydney which began meeting at 2 a.m. on Tuesdays in order to reach Chinese restaurant workers. This is the way we need to think. Where do we go next with the gospel? Who are the people who have not heard, and how can we reach them? Paul wrote Romans to put this on the agenda of our churches.

Pioneering does not necessarily mean going to some remote place. It is about what happens in our life every day. It is about whom you are going to sit next to on the bus – actually, it means deciding whether you are going to take the bus into town or drive your own car! If we are *'to boldly go where no one has been before,'* our church leaders need to think about freeing their people up so that they are not constantly in church and have time to make friends with non-Christians, and to share their Christian friends with their non-Christian friends.

Partnering

The third ingredient of mission is partnering. Paul tells the church at Rome:

> *'But now . . . since I have been longing for many years to see you, I plan to do so when I go to Spain. I hope to visit you while passing through, and to have you assist me on my journey there, after I have enjoyed your company for a while.'*
>
> (Romans 15:23-24)

We can see from other passages of Scripture that the phrase 'assist me on my journey' is almost a technical term. At the end of his letter to Titus Paul writes:

> *'As soon as I send Artemas or Tychicus to you, do your best to come to me at Nicopolis, because I have decided to winter there. Do everything you can to help Zenas the lawyer and Apollos on their way and see that they have everything they need.'*
>
> (Titus 3:12-13)

Zenas and Apollos were not freeloaders, but gospel workers who needed support. There was no central fund, so Paul lays it on the conscience of Titus to help them on their way, ensuring that they have all they need.

The apostle John uses similar language in his lovely little letter to his friend Gaius:

> *'Dear friend, you are faithful in what you are doing for the brothers, even though they are strangers to you. They have told the church about your love. You will do well to send them on their way in a manner worthy of God. It was for the sake of the Name that they went out, receiving no help from the pagans. We ought therefore to show hospitality to such men so that we may work together for the truth.'*
>
> (3 John 5-8)

Gaius was a Christian who could be relied on to help gospel workers on their way – unlike Diotrephes, the man who ruled the roost in the church: *'Diotrephes, who loves to be first, will have nothing to do with us . . . he refuses to welcome the brothers. He also stops those who want to do so and puts them out of the church'* (3 John 9-10). How many churches have been ruined by power brokers who hold the reins and allow nothing to happen unless their fingerprints are on it! Are you a Diotrephes or a Gaius, a help or a hindrance to the evangelisation of the world?

The apostle is looking forward to catching up with people in Rome. He has never been there before, but he already knows some of them because he has come across them elsewhere. Aquila and Priscilla were in Rome at the time, and you will recognise other familiar names in chapter 16. He has been praying for some of these people and receiving news of them, and he is looking forward to enjoying their company. When Paul tells the Roman church that he hopes they will assist him on his journey, he is not just asking for a bed for the night! Rather he is saying, *'The reason I'm coming to Rome is not just to enjoy your company. It's to plunder your church. I'm coming to recruit a team. I want you to be the new Antioch in Rome. I want to build a base for the evangelisation of the Western world.'*

There is a moving moment at the end of *Schindler's List*. Oskar Schindler had saved over twelve hundred Jews from certain death in the gas chambers by bribing Nazi officials to let them work in his munitions factory, and had bankrupted himself in the process. When the war is over and the allies are approaching, the Jews come with their letters of recommendation to the allies, telling of how this man has helped them. At this point Schindler breaks down: *'I could have done so much more!'* He points to his battered Mercedes, *'I could have sold that and saved ten more'*; he plucks out the solid gold pin from his lapel, *'This could have saved two more – I could have done so much more!'*

On that great day when we appear before the great white throne, is that what we will have to say? *'I could have done so much more! All those committees I have been on, so many minutes kept and hours wasted! All that money tied up in trust funds, and buildings that are no longer occupied! Why didn't we do something about it? Why didn't we use those resources to reach people for Christ? Why did I need two cars, that overseas holiday, five bathrooms, and an extension . . .? I could have done so much more!'*

When Paul talks to the Roman church about helping him on his journey, this is what he means. He is going to pick his team and take their best workers – hard workers, risk-takers (they are all there in chapter 16); and he wants the church's financial help too. Just as Antioch sent out Paul and Barnabas to travel around the eastern Mediterranean with the gospel, so now he wants Rome to partner with him and send him out with a team to Spain to evangelise the Western world. The question for us, then, is, Will I go or shall I stay? If I stay, then it must be to pay and to pray.

Praying

That brings me to the last point: praying. *'I urge you, brothers, by our Lord Jesus Christ and by the love of the Spirit, to join me in my struggle by praying to God for me'* (Romans 15:30). Praying is a struggle; it is hard work and does not come naturally to us. *'But I don't get anything out of the prayer meeting,'* you say. Who said you are supposed to get anything out of it? It is hard work, and you are supposed to put something into it. When the young man Joshua was fighting the battle down on the plain, Aaron and Hur were on the hill, holding up Moses' hands: *'As long as Moses held up his hands, the Israelites were winning'* (Exodus 17:11).

The story is told of someone who revisited a big Baptist church in Moscow after the end of the cold war. Noticing, in the vast congregation, row upon row of women dressed in black, he asked the pastor, *'Who are those ladies sitting up there, in black?' 'Ah,'* said the pastor, *'those are the women who prayed Communism out of Russia.'* These little old babushkas had no Kalashnikovs, but they had Bibles, and they prayed Communism out of Russia.

'Join with me in my struggle', says Paul. That is where the real work happens: nothing will be achieved otherwise. If you are a pastor, perhaps a young man in your first pastorate with lots of ideas, remember that nothing at all will happen unless you call on your people to join you in the struggle by praying for you.

It is interesting to note that those who know how to pray will be most solicitous of other people's prayers. An old friend told me of something that happened at Westminster Chapel when Dr Lloyd-Jones was ministering there. The Doctor would always attend the prayer meetings that were held before the preaching services at the Chapel. On one occasion he asked, *'Don't you appreciate my ministry?'* The person leading the prayer meeting said, *'Well, of course we do, Doctor.'* *'Then why don't you pray for me?'* *'Surely, Doctor, you don't need our prayers?'* *'Well,'* said the Doctor, *'you don't know me; you don't know me.'*

When William Carey went to India with the gospel, he wrote home to his friend Andrew Fuller, *'I am going into the pit, but you must hold the rope.'* Is your church prayer meeting holding the rope, or are you just taking a polite interest in some poor missionary who has sold up and gone off to the ends of the earth? Perhaps you enjoy getting an e-mail every now and again, but who is holding the rope? And do you pray for your pastor, or just complain about him?

Did God answer Paul's prayer requests? He is making three requests:

* to be rescued from his enemies
* that the Jewish believers in Jerusalem may accept the collection
* that he may come to Rome

> 'Pray that I may be rescued from the unbelievers in Judea and that my service in Jerusalem may be acceptable to the saints there, so that by God's will I may come to you with joy and together with you be refreshed.'
>
> (Romans 15:31-32)

The account in the book of Acts (chapters 21–27) shows us that God answered those prayers, but not quite in the way he was expecting. He went to Jerusalem with the money and was warmly received by the church, but the commander of the Roman troops had to rescue him from a lynch mob. His nephew visited him in the barracks with news that a contract had been taken out on his life, and so the Romans whisked him off to Caesarea, where he appeared before Felix, Festus and Agrippa – it is as though everyone was playing 'Pass the parcel' with him! But eventually God answered his prayer and he came to Rome – through trials and court appearances, shipwreck and snake bite, in chains and with all expenses paid by the emperor Nero!

God always answers prayer, but not always in the way we might expect. Perhaps the reason we do not pray is because we are afraid of what he might do if we pray about important, kingdom-centred things. He might just make us the answer to our own prayers. He might send our children or grandchildren to another part of the world, so that we will not see them again except on Skype. Remember what Mrs Beaver said to Susan: 'Aslan is not a tame lion.' Is that the sort of God you want – a boringly predictable God who is at your beck and call, and who just rubber-stamps the plans you have made when you show them to him? Or do you want a sovereignly interesting God who does all things according to his will? It is good to plan and have ambition, but our plans and ambitions must always be subject to the will of God.

Did Paul go to Spain? Nobody really knows. The last we see of him is that he is preaching the kingdom of God boldly in Rome without hindrance (Acts 28:31). He may have been in chains and under house arrest, but the gospel was without hindrance; it can penetrate anywhere.

To conclude

Paul has a priestly ministry: to proclaim Christ to the nations, to see the Gentiles set apart by the Holy Spirit, and to bring them as an offering to the God of Israel. In preaching the gospel and proclaiming Christ he is worshipping God.

Paul has a pioneer ministry, breaking new ground and boldly going where no one has been before. There is urgent need for us to do that. We need to ask, Where do we go next with the gospel? And we need to help one another to break new ground.

Such a ministry is perilous, fraught with danger. Whenever there is gospel advance, there will be fierce opposition. We need to feel Paul's heartbeat in this passage, to see the bigger picture, and to pray as never before, engaging in urgent, extraordinary prayer for the nations to be brought in and for the Jews to be converted.